Sounds

of

Feeling

By Kathryn Boice

Sounds
of
Feeling

Copyright by Kathryn Boice 1991

I.S.B.N. No. 09624811-2-2

Published by Silver Publications
a division of CRNW 1991
5215 West Clearwater Suite 107-25B
Kennewick, Washington 99336
(509) 783-3337 or FAX (509) 783-1838

All rights reserved. No part of this book may be reproduced in any form, electronic or mechanical, including photocopying, recording, or by any information storage and retrieval system now known or hereafter invented, without written permission from the publisher.

Kathryn Boice

Kathryn Boice

Kathryn was born Kathryn Margaret Weaver in Sweet Springs, Missouri in 1913. Having lost her mother at an early age, Kathryn and her sister and brother moved with their dad who was a school teacher. They also lived for a while with their "sainted" (Kathryn's term) grandmother in Arkansas. Growing up for Kathryn was an adventure of new homes in Missouri, Washington, and Arkansas.

Kathryn received her teaching certificate from the University of Arkansas at Fayetteville. She had a wonderful experience of Benton County and Washington County, Arkansas before relocating back to the state of Washington. She was married to William George Boice in 1936. Kathryn and Bill have three children, George, Billy, and Janelle. They raised their family in the Tri-Cities, Washington.

Kathryn's cultural and artistic talents are reflected in her children, as evidenced by the original illustrations created for this book by her daughter Janelle Goldbloom.

Kathryn is a long-standing member of Mid-Columbia Writers Association and has been published in: Tri-City Herald, The Oregonian (Portland), Tacoma News Tribune, Ideals, Book of Friendship-Ideals, Capper's Farmer, Denver Post, Seattle Post Intelligencer, Spokesman Review (Spokane), Centennial Celebration of Emily Dickinson's First Poetry Book, Wallula Poets, National DAR Magazine. Songs of the Columbia, was her first published book of poetry. The poem, Songs of the Columbia, included in this book, was selected to be featured in the Washington Centennial production of the Mid Columbia Symphony program of original music, poetry and art; reading by Kathryn Boice.

Kathryn's varied and colorful life-experience has brought a universality to her poetry. The reader can easily relate and understand the strong emotions exhibited in her poems. As her good friend, I like to compare Kathryn to Grandma's Lye Soap; neat, clean and with a bite.

Congratulations, Kathryn, for sharing your wonderful treasure book.
Jo Hollier
President
Mid-Columbia Writers Association

Publishers Notes

Whether you are young or young at heart, Kathryn's poetry quenches the depth and dimensions found in facets of experience.

Her poetry exposes raw feelings; feelings as real as life. Therefore the title, "Sounds of Feeling." You will experience laughter, love, emptiness, regret, irony, respect, honor, and of course, a great new insight to life itself.

Sometimes it takes great courage to share the intimacy of life.

We consider it a privilege to publish Sounds of Feeling. We trust you will enjoy this book as much as we did.

The Publisher

This book is dedicated
to
My husband Bill
and
My Children

SECOND SUNDAY IN MAY

*Blessed be
maternity
on this her day of days
when churches all
are wall to wall
bosoms and bouquets*

INTESTINAL FORTITUDE

*There comes a trial time
when pressed so hard
against the wall
endurance fails,
and broken,
       bleeding,
              beaten,
you, unconscious, fall.*

*Or else, when pushed so hard
by human will,
the wall gives 'way.
The mortar
breaks to crumbs
and hard
       bricks
              fall.*

SPRING HEDGE

Nor'westers blow forsythia gold
across the lawn to spend itself
into a brown extinction.

"An equinoctial violence,"
my salty sailor said,
"When days and nights swing
balanced on celestial verge of spring."

Seamen are most wise in certain lore
of stars and skies, but lax
in truth and promises on shore.

Beneath the clustered yellow bloom
he coaxed a pristine love
with bold caresses, indiscreet
as yesterday's forsythia.

LUNAR SONNET

Last night I watched Diana, maiden moon
       dip as she bathed in our back pasture pond.
       She pressed the bank of fern and kissed a frond
that bent to catch the floating orange balloon.
A night bird sang an evening mating tune
       to his love in a red haw bush beyond
       the pool, then silenced for her to respond.
On a wind wake swayed the golden orb. Soon
the sun, in glory, master of the sky,
       would light the earth. With his all-seeing eye
       he'd think her up to some nocturnal wrong.
Wrapped in a froth of cloud, she rose on high.
Behold her - dim, misshapen, faded. Why?
Had she played in our pasture pond too long?

CHANGE

The old wag said
(I quote)
"Beware the Ides of love.
When passions pall
      Monotony,
             Monogamy, and
                    Marriage all
are one with boredom

Flash backs of pleasures past
meld into a future cauldron
a body wrinkled and unsure
a mind of tangled tensions

In guilt nouveau you grasp at
tight-rope fringe to stay
erosion's nearing brink."
(unquote)

Instead of an insatiate bed
I've found a surrogate;
I think:
      Kaleidoscope of
        Cruises,
             Facelifts,
Diamonds and Mink.

SEPARATION

*One evening we came upon this;
a wild fox tearing at her wound,
clawing pain to ease pain.*

. . . . . .

*Pressing at helpless tears,
I watch. She fingers
photographs and gathers
memories and years
into two separate
entities of finality;
His and Hers.*

IN AN ORCHARD

*So basic
the apple orchard is,
where amber sun drips
through September haze
like summer honey
from wild bees
upon prolific limbs.*

*Familiar with a feminine
desire and appetite,
I swallow with a
grain of salt the story
that she taunted him
to take the initial bite.
Fruition of the Word
exacts supremely more
from me than those
chance pippin stones.*

*I comprehend a
universal consciousness
beyond my meager own.
Let my divining nostrils
fill with heavy scent
of sin original.*

*So basic
the apple orchard is.*

FIDDLER'S CHOICE

Bow to your partner.
Honor your corner.

Allemande left a white oak tree
Rail fence form a ring
Dogwood sashay up the draw
Sumac pigeon wing
Redbud circle sassafras
Promenade the hill
*Bodark lead a holler stump
Behind the water mill
Honeysuckle do-ce-do
Circle 'round the moon.
Arkansas pays the fiddler
When April calls the tune.

Keeno.

* bois d' arc

EVANGELIST'S DAUGHTER

Having heard them all, the
"Thou Shalt Not's",
I watch the dancers
sway in sin while
my own 'foot washed' toes
tap out the tune.

At 'spin the bottle',
when it points my way
I cough, and blush, and
turn my face. These
sheltered shoulders yearn
to feel a muscled arm without
a guilty 'fall from grace'.

My mind programmed
for "predestination" is
ignited by the fire of Hell
with flames that rivers of
immersion cannot quell.

Why count off numbered laws
to pester, nettle, and annoy
when one staunch
Calvinist commandment
could have said it all?

"Thou shalt not enjoy".

KINSHIP

*My headlight
caught reflected hurt
in animal eyes.*

*I braked to a stop.
The doe dragged
her wounded leg
across two lanes
of macadam.*

*A timid creature,
never meant to vie
with horsepower.*

*She reached the dark
shoulder of the road.*

*One trusting glance back,
half jumped and half fell
into thicket.*

*I heard the sound of
breaking plant growth and
knew she was alive.*

*How is it with animals?
Is an injured, returning,
welcomed into a helpful herd,
or left alone to heal?
To die?*

*Silence closed around me.
Starting the car's engine,
I pressed into the night.
I, too, am limping home.*

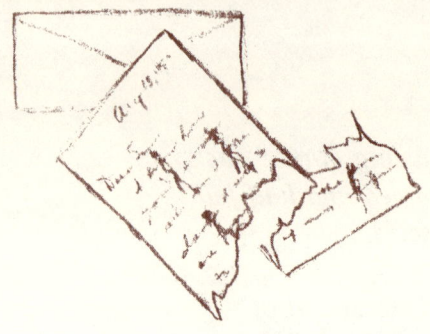

SO SILENTLY A HEARTBREAK

So silently a heartbreak comes.
There is no cracking of the bone,
No crashing sound -
No tearing flesh nor spurt of blood,
No gaping wound.

So silently a heartbreak comes
With quiet tears
That no-one sees the ugly scar
and no-one hears.

But pain, throughout the dark of night
And into dawn
Gnaws, until alone you cry with sense
and feeling gone.
So silently a heartbreak comes.

FRIENDSHIP

Friendship is a fragile thing,
A gossamer web, a fairy wing.
Yet all the chains contrived by man
Can never bind as friendship can.

AN OBSERVATION

Frustration, Dear, is heaven-sent.
We'd have no pearls if oysters were content.

PERCEPTION

He knows not the meaning of darkness
Who has seen no glimmer of light.

By our sight we measure our blindness
And by dawn the length of our night.

ARTIST

*The same great God who
hurls the planets and the stars,
paints butterflies.*

DREAMS

*My dreams, kite colored,
fly like wild clouds in a wind.
I hold tight the string.*

NEWSPAPER

*Monday morning, I
toss out old news, ads, funnies
and Sunday's acquired guilt.*

STREET-WISE

*What miracle wrought
this tender blade of grass to
split the macadam?*

HAIKU

DODDER

*We called it love-vine, yesterday
when we were children, and in play
tied golden tendrils into things
like necklaces and wedding rings -
too full of laughter to have watched
how it possessed each life it touched,
how tender fingers bound and bent
to choke the source of nourishment.*

JUNE GAME

My best of craft and feathers
shaped the lure.
My casting was superb,
my calculated aim was sure.

The trusty hook is set!
I play the line.
He flashes in one final leap!
All mine.
Enclose him in the net.

The sport is done and
I am left to grapple with
the catch I've won.

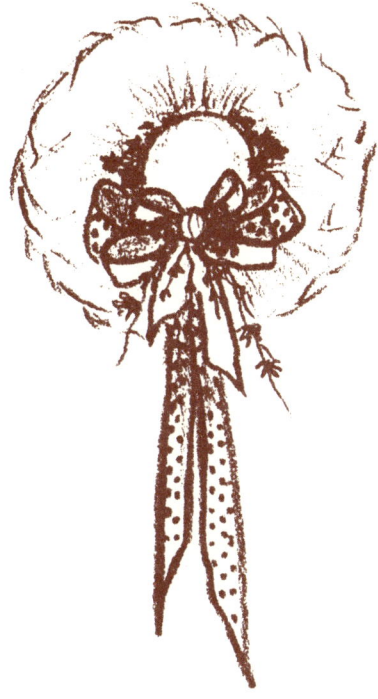

COLLAGE FOR 11 A.M.

Her Easter bonnet so botanically pure
only the honeybee knows for sure

Children in raiment all reeking with new
bloom psychedelic along the pew

A husband with posture uncomfortably straight
out seasoned by a collection plate

Kind Father, do grant them a spiritual lift
to last 'til December twenty-fifth.

SPARROW AT THE WINDOW

*You dart so madly
thrusting yourself against the pane,
falling stunned to ground
below - then trying it again.*

*How warped the picture
through the glass - that you who fly about
so free - would want inside
and I so desperately want out.*

REVISION

The white heat of a midnight flame
fires dross from crucibles that hold
the findings of a mind and soul
to free a thread of poet's gold.

AND ANOTHER

*I held my cup of
wanderlust and stars -
not knowing thirst -
until you paused
to fill it to the brim.*

*We laughed
throughout the night
and quaffed
the effervescence
rim on rim.*

*Now thirst
unquenchable I know
from gilded cups
that overflow
with emptiness.*

CONCH

*You lay half buried in the sand -
barnacle-encrusted,
from an ocean floor.*

*What tumult tossed you here
onto my posted, "Private" shore?*

*I hold this rose-tipped spiral
to my land-locked ear.*

*I am Ulysses, evermore seduced
by siren song and tempest roar.*

VALENTINE BY COMPUTER

*Unused software,
a maze of dreams
waiting for my touch.*

*Is love so complicated?
The salesman said,
"It will be easy,
errors are self-rectified."*

All magic.

*The psyche baffles at old
heart-created phrases,
passe' and unprocessed
by the brain.*

*On what keys or codes
must fumbling fingers
light to conjure something
scented, laced with ribbon,
to be kissed gently
in the night?*

JUNE

*Most adequate was my world of prose
until I watched a virgin rose
unfold her petals to the bee.*

*Thanks, God, for
    Love and Poetry.*

FEBRUARY 15th.

Valentines:
*   Half price,*
candy, ribbon, lace.
Cupids with their arrows
are passe'.

*   I say*
Love is mobile and
with built-in obsolescence.
The shelf life of your heart
was yesterday.

REVERIE

Oh, had I a cache of time
where I could resurrect
a long neglected rhyme,
one I had hidden
on a summer day
        a laugh, a lilt, a rondelet.

A compliment from you,
gift wrapped in memory
with warning apt to
        "handle carefully"

The shadows whisper
and I know
beyond cold candle ash
there is a glow of presence
in this silent room,
a wisp of aura
through the gloom,
heart to heart
        and then...

Oh..., could I call back the
hours and do it all over again.

THE FALL

Eve bowed her head.
Shame coiled around her shoulders,
cold as snake skin.

Sweet fruit soured bitter on
her tongue. Flowers and tall
grasses withered at her touch.

The strong one whom she loved
had cast the blame on her.

God, what a heritage
for her daughters.

FOREVER, BELOVED

*Trees mirrored in this season's lake
Are like love letters several summers old.
Unseen dimensions caused by time
and light remake
The budding promises they hold.*

*If truth is subject to our years
Reflected phrases will unshape and feel
Beyond a length and breadth,
through boundary of fears,
Awareness with today's tight focus real.*

SPRING LOVE

*Too early yet to sow
Old timers say "Late frost
You are too young to know."*

*I only know that now
the earth is moist and
sweet*

responsive to the plow.

LIB

*Perhaps I could have had
the muscled body or
male idiom of the
intellectual brain,
but if my consequence
is merely co-existence
the trauma of the rib
has been in vain.
This aura soul I buy
instead of brawn or bawdy
and if I give more in
the barter than receive -
my punishment -
mystique and intuition.
This is the price I pay for being Eve.*

ROSEBUD

*Rosebud - velvet soft
and invitation scarlet,
your thorns prick my thumb.*

ELEGY BEFORE DAWN

*She-ah-beth stepped
into the jungle stream. She waded
through dark water as it pushed
against her torrid thighs. She stood deep
in the flow and felt fresh eddies cool
the fever in her breast.*

*Her ebon fingers
loosened knotted reeds that held
a crippled weight upon her back.
The burden slipped into the swirling
wave and knelling currents swelled
to drown the final gasp.*

*Sweet water washed
the salt tears from her face. The river
poured its sacrament upon her head.
She stretched her clean hands
empty to the sky and walked unbowed
the channel's brackish edge.*

*A new day played
across the sultry east. She knew
her husband would be rising
from his mat. She-ah-beth's god had been
appeased and next year's babe would be
to keep. Strong-limbed and straight.*

SHEEPMAN'S WIFE

Grudgingly, without thought for human stomachs,
she pours greasy gravy into the big cracked bowl
and piles high the fried potatoes on the platter.
She splashes full of bitter brew
the crock-cups used for coffee.
Above the swearing supper-talk of men
she hears a new lamb bleating
and birth cry of the ewe.
Far into the night she kneels upon the hay.
With hands that have felt death and birth,
she holds a baby lamb.

GARDEN PERFIDY

*The white butterflies
caress the green cabbage plants.
June's love. August's worms.*

INTERIM

*Old dog sleeps before the fire
and dreams of those crisp autumn days
in younger years
when breed and blood
arose to meet the challenge
of the hunt. Her ears
twitch and her muscles flex.
Does she remember all those pups
she nursed and taught
to follow scent,
to tree the wiley coon
or point the bird? Caught
in complexities of years,
we wait out together here
this twilight span
between our last
tramp and those greater hunts to
come - for dog and man.*

CHRISTMAS CACOPHANY

*Between white sky snow
and black street slush
fenders bend,
traffic tempers flare,
shrieking sirens blow,
while electronic anthems blare,
"Peace on Earth."*

CHRISTMAS 1970

*When star-song splits the ether sphere
with, "Peace, goodwill to men",
when children voices carol clear
an, "Ave and amen",
when hearts and hearths share love and cheer,
it's Christmas time again.*

CHRISTMAS 1980

I wish you miracles:
Skies that sing Messiah's birth,
stars to guide the wise, the worth
of hallowed hearths and bells that ring
of "Peace on earth."
I wish you Christmas.

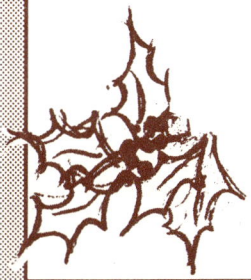

FESTIVAL OF LIGHT

*In her homestead shack my mother
lit a candle and placed the circle
of light on the organ,
pump organ brought by rail
from her childhood home
in Missouri.*

*Small glow
against a wilderness
       of wind,
              and sand,
                      and night.*

*There were papers to grade from her
school, a stronghold of learning,
one-room learning for pioneer children
and native Navajo.*

*A year to prove her land,
       new home,
             new state,
                   New Mexico.*

*Through wars and depressions,
through sheep and cattle,
by dawn's first ray and Lantern beam
I held to this land,   to this dream.*

Then came oil!

*In memory of my mother
are Lights in the mission church,
showers of heavenly halos with switches,
           rheostats,
                 controls, and
                       Many candle power.*

CHRISTMAS EVE

*New snow exalts the garbage pit
into a holy shrine.*

*The moonlight haloed fence posts
stand as angel choirs, divine.
A worry-weighted world is
tuned to cosmic carolings
and human hearts, awe-hushed
await the miracle that Bethlehem brings.*

CONTENTMENT

I need not search beyond the distant stars and skies
For some ethereal Paradise.

Earth-eyes, that in each sunrise deity behold,
Would blinded be by streets of shining gold.
And music of celestial harps fall flat upon the ear
That is atune to larks across the mere.

These feet that walk behind a plow in April loam
Within white, pearly gates would never feel at home.

SPECTRUM

*Through sanctity of stained glass
with its verdant vine,
its purple fleur-de-lis,
and scarlet rose,
the white-robed bishop
views his hexagon of
cosmic blue.*

*He pours sacramental wine
and blesses those who dip
unleavened bread.
Steeped in his dedicated holiness
he moves through scent of
ritual brazier and
candles of contrition.*

*Within this summit edifice,
he monotones the prayers, unseeing
mass polluted swamps below
where yellowed heads of
odoriferous skunk cabbages
prolifically grow.*

SUNDAY AT MT. RAINIER

*Indian shaped his deity
into a mountain's majesty
while white men, civilized, insist
God's Catholic,
    Jew, or
        Methodist.*

THE CONSTANT BEAM

Through complex condominiums,
Safe-guarded by electric eye,
Through strata of society
Where precinct prejudices lie;

The Star with laser sureness shows
A manger babe in swaddling clothes.

INVITATION

Come,
Walk with me to Bethlehem
across the sands tonight
a desert breeze is sweet with myrrh
    Our guiding star is bright.

We hear the heavenly chorus sing
"Glory to God on High"
    While shepherds, awe struck,
    guard their sheep and watch
    as we pass by.
We see the milling midnight crowd
around a donkey shed
And we in adoration kneel
before the Manger Bed.

1st SAMUEL 2:19

*Hannah wondered if she had allowed
enough for length of sleeve
and shoulder width.
Boys grow so tall in just a year.
She tested strength of warp and woof
and matched the pattern in the weave.
She threaded love into each seam
with quiet care for body need of warmth
beyond blind Eli and the dream.
She made a hem deep to a changing day
and bound together edges that might fray
or bare.
Thus mothers sew for growing boys
the robes God's holy prophets wear.*

CYCLE

When I was six,
I wrestled with new knowledge,
shaking my belief
in Good Saint Nick.
Embarrassed by my fouled-up fantasy,
I vowed to stick
to scientific fact.
Each season, surer
I became, that goodwill was
a hoax hatched in
the merchant guild
to line the profiteering
pocket and bring
silver, jingle-belling
to the till.

But now, at forty-six,
I comprehend a truth
I doubted in my youth, because
a Christmas grandchild
turned this egoistic self
into a Santa Claus.

FROM A SHAKER DIARY

*Tuesday
will never be the same again.
Always it just follows Monday.
The washin' done, I iron,
and when the churnin's over,
call upon the shut-ins.*

Never anythin' outstanding about Tuesday.

*Wednesday, a girl can roll her hair in rags
and, with her quiltin' stitches,
think about prayer meetin' night.*

*Other days are shortened by the bakin'
and the Bible readin'.*

*Saturday is market day and
scrubbin' for the Sabbath.*

*Sunday, pious in my pew, I try
to concentrate upon the preachin'.
Instead of sorrowin' for sin,
my flighty mind forms truant memories
of porch steps shadowed from a peepin' moon,
and sweet excitement when
his sturdy hand held mine.*

*On Tuesday, he had only come to buy
a pound of butter.*

I hope it doesn't last the week!

THE SUNDAY AUCTION

Rapped on my compromising conscience,
    "Once, twice," the voice of the
colonel - auctioneer
catapulted through the gray
waves of cigarette smoke.
    "Three times; going, going,"
blurred in stereo.

A distant church bell beckoned.
    "Next Sunday," I bargained,
    "I'll be in church next Sunday."
Somewhere I had heard,
    'The road to Hell is paved
    with good intentions.'

    "Going, going, for twenty-five,
    do I hear thirty,"
the auctioneer coerced the anxious crowd,
    "for this exquisite pane of
    antique stained glass?"

    "Thirty," I called,
waving my auction number high.

    "Once, twice, three times,
    and sold for thirty dollars."

His gavel hit the podium.
I counted out the thirty I had bid.

Conscience, like fine glass,
is bartered, a small piece at a time.

PRAYER FOR A BOWHEAD HUNTER

*Through the thick hours of night
she holds aloft the vessels
with the water pure, until
the crescent moon slips into sight
and prays,*
> *"Great Allingnuk,
> forever dweller of the moon".*

*Her soul is purified, her penitences done.
This is the whaler's moon.*
> *"Before the first spring sunlight
> thaws the dawn,
> tip high the golden spoon,
> hold fast the sea".*

This is the whaler's moon.
> *"The frozen tundra yields so soon
> to hoof of caribou.
> Great Allingnuk, in ice-fringed
> Arctic splendor surely move
> across the cracking borealis
> and bring him safely home".*

This is the whaler's moon.

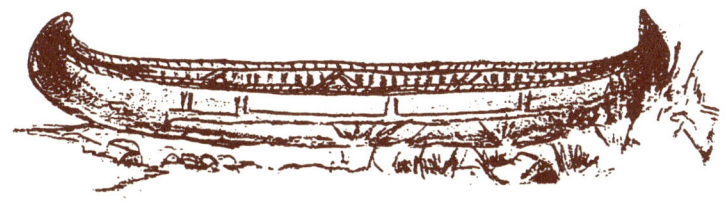

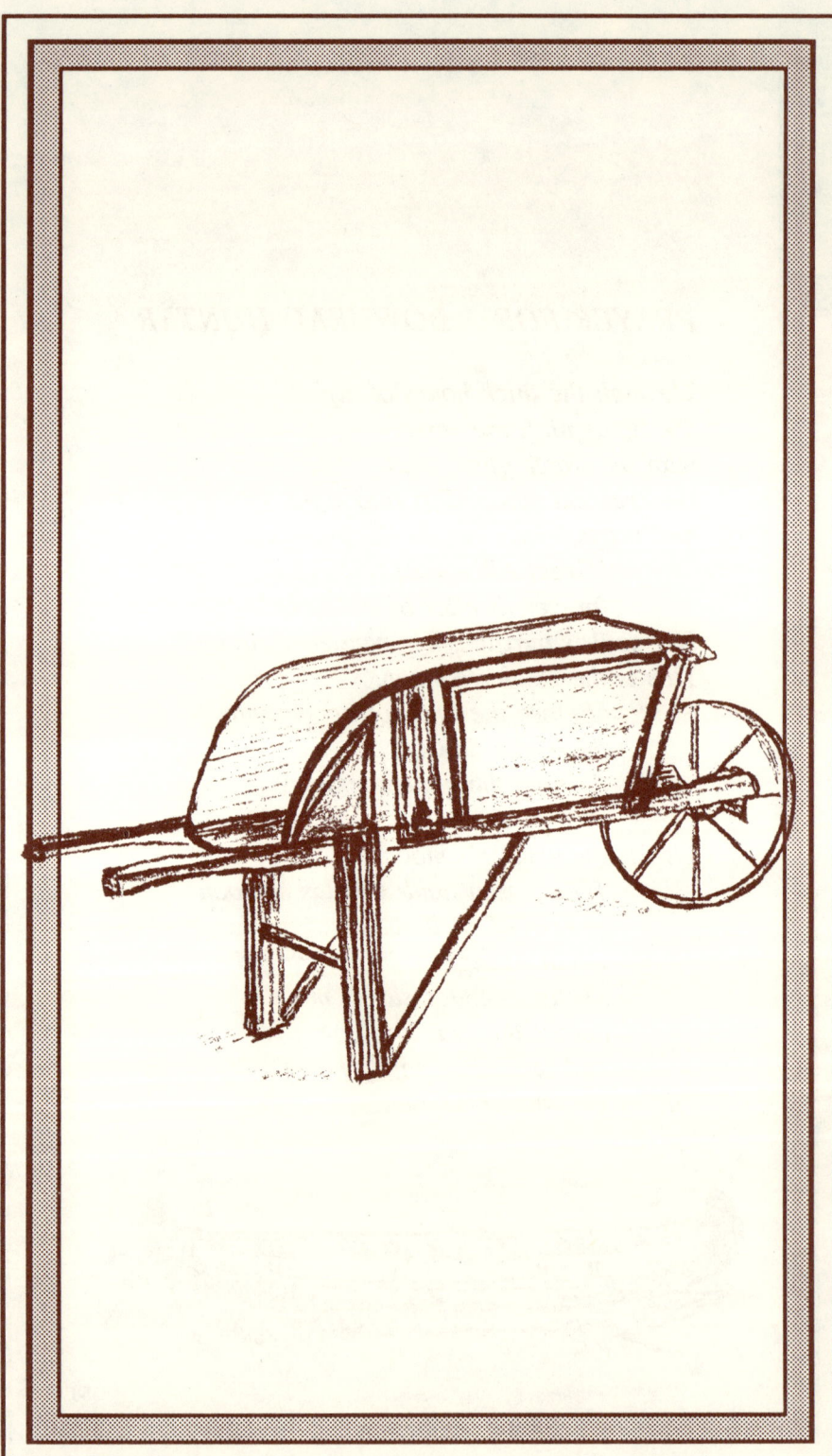

SALISBURY

On moonlit plains the hooded
Druids chant in single file
with twigs, rosemary,
black thorn and mistletoe.
Sharp fingers of gray smoke,
stone honed and bitter
with fresh scent of sloe
feel out the crevices in
rock to free a witch's
spell of woe.

The whetted winds from muted
centuries of sacrifice and rites
inscribe an epitaph on
lintel sills and drone
of sorcery through hallowed nights
across the henge to
Wilshire hills.

GREAT GRANDFATHER

Tells me legends that his
great grandfather told him of
    animals with feathers,
    beasts that talk, and
    mountains that belch fire.

His blind eyes look to the west
as he follows the sun, turning
his bare scrawny back to
the last warm rays.

Great grandfather talks,
summoning spirits
from the sage brush root
into the figure he is creating

He inhales sharp scent from the acrid
fibrous grain he thumbs.
A primitive head takes shape
under the flint scraper.
No human motions are lost as
they flow into the patina of a pony,
a pony with phantom feathers as
thin as mist.

Eastern sky pushes day into darkness
The carver finishes the two supporting bird legs.

Great grandfather traces his bone
fingers through my hair and pins
my braid with prongs of the horse bird.

I dance and plumes rise and fall into
rhythms from coyote song,
        ancient tom-toms and
        spirits of mountains
        on fire.

Great grandfather sleeps

CELILO - REQUIEM FOR A RACE

Above an inundated heritage
the knelling sounds.
White mists conceal the judgement balances.
The chiefs of ancient feast
and flooded fishing grounds
sought right in treaty,
> "As long as suns rise in the east
> and rivers meet the sea
> wampum will not buy this wauna place,
> the site shall be as it was with
> our fathers".

No more the Wishrams moccasined
against a slippery face of rock
stand spear poised for predestined fish,
nor salmon silver in a stimulus to spawn
leap cascades and crowd each other
in the run. No acrid smoke of alder
drying racks of sweet Chinook
nor pemmican
red pounded in the sun.

> Gray is the Great, Great Oregon
> and dammed and dammed.

Above an inundated heritage,
Celilo - Requiem for a race.

DIMENSION

*Sunrise to sunset,
dark to first light.
Man has measured,
metered, minimized
his hours to day and night.
The same for Sweitzer,
Homer, Michelangelo,
or Judas. Sands sift out
our Calvaries and know
the time for resurrection.
A twenty-four hour day can be
a nothing or eternity.*

FOR LENT

Lord,
Through centuries of dawn
a chanticleer cries challenges,
denials,
fears, that
Peter never dreamed of.

We gamble gold,
not ours
or Caesar's.
We probe and tamper
with a time of
life and death. We
play at god in games with galaxies.

Match strength of muscle
to our spirit fiber,
Lord,
and wisdom
for decisions that
will call from star to star,

"We knew Him, Yes, We knew Him".

THE DAY WE BURIED CALLIE

Monday's clouds hung bleached and high,
spread horizontal on a bluing sky
like white folks linen sheets
and lace-bound underwear,
billowing sweet-scented in the apple-blossom air.

Inside the rough pine chest her washboard hands
lay still across a sunken breast.
A smile glowed on her wrinkled face,
born of belief and faith as sure
and strong as home-made soap,
that she would meet her Maker
in the place and hour prepared for her
beyond this scope of suds and rinse and scour,
eternal in a Heaven of white marble mansions
and alabaster towers:

no weariness, no stalking fear, no
'Colored Entrance in the Rear'.

PAROCHIAL

*I do not need to justify
my righteousness, my name,
my attributes. It was my wax,
my match, my flame.
I trimmed the wick and watched
to shelter it from breezes that would blow
the haloed incandescence
from its glow.
I fanned it when it flickered
through the threatening night
and guarded shine
from those who would ignite
unworthy rush from mine,
for fear a lesser light
would let me stumble in the gloom.
Engrossed with the resplendent flush
of circled brilliance in the room
these out-of-focus eyes
had followed a too feeble ray.*

*Beyond my wall, the sun had risen
and I had missed the miracle of a day.*

Night Poem

Words written in the dark are as bird tracks in wet sand. Marks by phantom quills that drawn distort beneath the microscopic brilliance of the sun. Yet critics, scrutinizing, analyzing, technique-izing words, cannot obliterate reality of truth and birds.

VALDEZ

Unlike old mills of the
proverbial gods that grind
so..slowly but oh so...
exceedingly fine.
        the wheels of progress whine
        or squeal a deafening
        decimeter to the ear,
        accelerate late R.P.M.'s
                misguided desecrations
                foul the rim of
                primal Arctic air.

Unlike her kind, who known for
their amusing way,
dive to crack the shells
on rocky ocean floor and
dine on hidden albacore
        a lone otter swims a
        labored back stroke,
        her oil soaked baby lying
        dead upon her breast
                Today's contest is no game
                for play or quest of food.
Silently she slips
beneath an unctuous
scum of crude.

FOR VANCE

who called our attention
to a burl which he said'
    "Looks like a cat
    crouched upon that birdhouse
    in the maple tree."

We other three
saw nothing but an awkward
whorl of wood, mis-shapen rings
faulted by a mythic Pan.

Vance pointed out the ears,
the nose, the
salivating mouth.

    We tapped our foreheads
    with our mocking fingers,
    making 'Sunday picnic' fun
    of him and his Picasso type
    feline carnivorous.

The robins and the junkoes
gossiped, twittering their babel songs
while flying in and out
among the Sycamore and Oak.

I didn't tell, but I
had noticed that
not one feathered troubador
would venture near the sylvan shade
where waiting sat
Vance's anticipating cat.

GRAND CANYON HOLIDAY

While I stir supper in an open pot
at seven thousand feet,
an altitude most surely not
the best for cooking beans - complete -
my eldest in her tie-dyed jeans
takes basketry to split and twist
the native reeds. My next
shapes terra cotta to a bowl
and thumbs mud beads.
Commuting maze has gained its goal
and brought my husband
fifteen days - and pay.
The measured circle of success
is whole by status rule.
He jogs precariously the narrow rim
astride a mule.

TO A RUNAWAY RETURNING

To mend a breaking nest
I fit the fragment stem and string
where growing urge strained boundaries
too stringent for a trying wing.

I've cried out nights of weaving thatch,
"Pray God it holds," and spinning flax,
my bleeding fingers numbly raw,
until a thread of dawn shows
skeins of gold abundance
over floor that once
held naked straw.

FROM COUNTY HOSPITAL ROOM 202

through senile eyes
milky with anesthesia
I watch the few remaining leaves
let go their sterile stems
in unprotesting hush
from sapless limbs
before the freeze.

no nature stirs her spheres
with exit pleasantries
nor encores summer's mirth
better to have danced the
whirl of blaze october
than to lie numb on frozen
earth.

UPON BEING COMMITTED

--or maybe I was shoved.
I hear them talking,
*   "Just another one who*
*   fell through the cracks".*
I feel no slivers, no barbs.

Could it have happened slowly,
like sand flowing through the glass,
grain after grain after final grain
before the hourly turning?

How could they not know
the whole world has turned over and
I am the only one
*   on top.*

THE EARLY BIRD

*A shaft of blinding sunlight
peirced the early morning haze
windshields glared in golds,
and flames of red set skies ablaze.*

*Brakes, squealed, the bumper -
bumper traffic slowed.
Upon my steering wheel
impatient fingers tapped out
morse-type codes.*

*The gray gulls faded in the mists
and flying, shrieked as happy
children playing hide and seek.*

*But one lay, a majenta pool upon
a frosty asphalt street,
feathers tread marked, the worm
still wriggling in her beak.*

FISHING VILLAGE

*I like the certain strength
of sea-coast towns
where character of salt
and swarthiness abound,
where clapboard cottages
cling, half to the cliff
and half to sand -
a part of sea, yet
anchored to the land;
where jetty arms hold safe
a spindrift haven
for the men who have
their way with ship
      and sea
            and maid*

NOT WITHOUT HONOR EXCEPT

*The Fermi children show Enrico
sums and sciences from school;
and Mrs. Chippendale berates her Tom
to mend the milking stool.*

DANDELION WINE

*Dandelion wine;
pungent remembrance of loam,
bitter to swallow.*

SNOW

*A handful of snow.
Chaste, mystic shapes to cherish
drip through my fingers.*

BEACH HOUSE

The first storm,
sudden - unannounced
raged from the sea
to force its fury

on my strip of shore.
Tempestuous attacks
tore board from board and
twisted to unnatural shapes
the things most loved.
I picked among debris
of broken glass,
salvaging here and there
a piece to savor - precious,
spared by the assault of wrath.
Each succeeding storm
found less to satisfy
its blasphemy.

*A strange love holds flesh
to this bleak stretch of sand
where every spell of calm
breeds turbulence - and
where the spirit long ago
has fled to safer zone.*

*One meets storm better
unencumbered.*

TO A DANDELION

Above the grass you stood
Straight-stemmed,
Your once-gold crown
Now silver-starred
Within my finger tips
Almost-
I came too close.

THROUGH A JANUARY WINDOW

Undisciplined,
the swirls of powdered snow
play ring around, around,
and fall in phantom fantasies
upon a sleeping ground.

The sky, bereft
of flake and feather flurry
sags, limbo gray on white.
Horizons mute disputed boundaries
and ease abbreviated day
into extended night.

GINGKO TREE

*Your fans of Canton crepe
have winnowed for a season
the slanted sun and oriented shade.
Now north-blown breezes shape
to horizontal bareness
a gentle jasper and belated jade.*

*My wind bells chime a call
from dynasties of sages,
gray-bearded by philosophies retold.
Their words beyond the wall
wrote wisdom into beauty
translated on thick leaves
of gingko gold.*

CANNIBALISM

Uncle Julius
reads the evening Herald,
devouring sheriff sales,
bankruptcies,
digesting the 'last rites'
of competition gone 'belly up'.

Like a New Guinea warrior
consuming the warm flesh
of a defeated enemy,
Uncle Julius salivates,
absorbing adversary strength
into the body of the victor.

The alchemy of transmutation!

TO MA BELL... REACH OUT

When the last wire crawls into earth,
where do the sparrows sit, who
wrap their feet around the warmth
of winter gossip down the line?

Can children mete unmeasured boredom
through the boundless zone of summertime?
What heavenly pitch pipe tunes romance
among pale cumuli or zings the wind?

Who ties the farmstead to a town
beyond some other distant dawn?
Where do the shadows shrink to dial noon,
and can some hidden magic sigh a phrase of
silver lining to
                      "Goodbye"?

DECORATION DAY

By dawn, bouquets
were loaded on the wagon
and shaded from a later sun -
for memory of those
'Gone, but not forgotten'.

Children, with mute awareness
of the hour, were wrapped in
interrupted dreams and
patchwork quilts.

Crocks of potato salad,
thick sandwiches of buttered bread
and baskets of fried chicken
swayed as in a ship's hold,
with motion of the ride.

Wheels rumbled over silent sod,
so dearly won in bloody turns by
Blue and Gray.
Each year we counted fewer
that remembered why some plots
were marked with stars and stripes, while
on other mounds Confederate banners waved.

All hats removed - as families
found their stones of,
'Gone to be With Jesus',
'Our Sainted Brother', or
'For God and Country'.

We touched history with grandparents
through fevers, floods and wars,
hard winters and the answer
we accepted, 'God knows best'.

Food was spread and shared,
somber speeches - promising a
'Better life beyond'.
Tears and 'Goodbyes'.

Toward home the horses pulled a
wagon filled with remembering.

I pondered if the dead were better
for our 'Bitter Sweet'.
I knew the living were.

TRAVELOGUE

They show us slides
of their summer rides,
plus movies they made themselves,
but we really know
the places they go
by the towels on their bathroom shelves.

AT HONEST JOHN'S

The old man walked around the Chevy pickup,
kicked all four tires and thumped the spare.
He checked the speedometer, the fan, the carburetor,
hassled by the young 'ready-teddy' salesman,
told him of the REO he once owned,
"Before you were born, sonny;
they just don't make 'em like that no more."

Whing! tobacco spew hit a polished hub-cap.
"Tell ya, boy, your price is way too high,
figurin' it's cash,
I'll give ya
half the sticker price."

Proud of his shrewdness, he let go
a long, straight line of nicotine into an ant hill.
The boss called above the static on the loudspeaker,
"I just sold the pickup."

The old man sputtered something about being first,
but ready-teddy shrugged,
"Kicking and spitting is probably the story of his life;
they just don't make 'em like that no more."

PARABLE

*Five times each day
Abdul,
prostrated in prayer,
petitioned Allah
to grant a magic carpet
to bear him away to
some Elysian isle,
beyond*
       *the confines of his
       mother's aged hut
       that smacked of poverty
       and boiling fish;*
beyond
       *the urgings of his wife,
       monotonous and
       steady as the one-toned
       wind chime hanging from
       their twisted olive tree;*
beyond
       *the stone-walled city that
       choked him like the
       tourniquet above
       the snake bite
       on his father's leg,
       before the old man died.*

*Allah heard
and granted Abdul his desire.*

*Semitic night dissolved
into a blaze of eastern sunrise,
like treacle in hot brew,
while an elated Abdul rose
unfettered as a skylark
singing to a summer dawn
and floated free upon
his wingless tapestry.*

Above

>*the thick perfume that once
had lured him to the
shadowed alley with its
cribs of prostitutes;*

above

>*the haggling of bazaars,
the begging Bedouins and
pungent camel dung;*

above

>*the sprinkled smells where
censers drown the smoke from
Holy morning sacrifice.*

*Abdul's nostrils swelled
with scent of cinnamon
on a breeze from some
far-off windward paradise.*

*Alone with exotic
air and the imaginings
of siren song, he soared,
not knowing, as he glided over
church yards and
ancient sandarac,
a fringe of thread had caught
upon a parapet.*

*Held by the spire, unraveling
began - row after row as
Abdul flew.*

*He sat cross-limbed,
self-satisfied that Allah
had chosen to bestow on him
this blessed gift,
unconscious that around his
dormant feet were Persian
patterns disappearing.*

*When Abdul sensed his rug
diminishing, he shrieked a
plea to Allah. He bargained
prayer with ravings of a
frenzied mendicant.
He tried to turn the
magic carpet back to home.
He listed, leaned and pulled
at Oriental salvage.
The fabric yawed, it rolled,
it pitched and with each motion
smaller grew.*

Gone was the ecstasy of flight!

*Deserted by his philanthropic
god, Abdul caught at
wayward threads and
still the warp and woof
unraveled.*

*As ship-wrecked sailors
grasp at floating straw,
he desperately clung to
that last fiber strand.
He felt the vacuous
experience of descent and
in a flash remembered how
he once tossed a
fledgling sparrow
to the ground.*

*The ageless sea closed over
Abdul as he drowned.*

PRUNE PICKER

Because I was behind on my tight schedule
I drove along the ditch bank to my friend's
home, through the orchard instead of taking
the extra mile and a half by the country
road.

I inhaled a memory of deliciously sweet fruit
I had bought here years ago. Abundance weighted
every limb.

Breaking the car to a sudden stop I sat choking
on the dust that overtook me. Parked in the
narrow way ahead was an aged and wear beaten
pickup.

I bore down on my late model horn. After a second
blast I heard a "Hullo." He came from between two
rows of purple heavy trees; his canvas picking bag
swung 'round his waist.

Ancestry of canoeing showed in his walk. Wrinkles
eroded the terra cotta skin and thick black hair
tangled below a frayed broken straw hat.

His yellow decaying teeth were those of the salmon
eating Klickitats. He stood straight from the
ground to his broad shoulders, then bent forward
like an arrow that had been shot into something
immovable.

His smile broke slow, sincere.
"I thought you might like some ripe prunes."
He eased the plump fruit from his good arm
to the seat of my car.

His other, a stub hung as ragged as his torn
off shirt sleeve; a tattooed heart with
"Love" and half an American flag remained.

As he opened the creaking door to his truck
he added, "I hope I haven't taken too much
of your time, lady."

"That's O.K," I called, but underneath my
breath: "I hope I haven't taken too much
of yours, sir."

LESSON IN ORTHOGRAPHY

*At Sunday School
we filled a missionary barrel
and each one wrote a letter
to another Christian boy or girl,
copying with fourth-grade hands
the word C-O-R-E-A.
I never knew if this was the
accepted way or merely
teacher unfamiliarity
with other lands.*

*I know now to spell it with a K.
I traced it with my fingers
in a granite stone today.*

JERSEY BULL CALF

*Snow still leans against the north side
of the barn in dirty fringe and wind
blows at the widening cracks where hay
is stacked when winter-time begins.
The pungence of warm blood and
body smell of cow are thick within
the stall. New daylight feels its way
through loft to spotted wall. Her bovine
eyes examine him and soft -
so soft the sound, he feels it more than
hears, and pushes for that first warm
sustenance. He is of value here
where love is a rough cow lick.*

NORTH DAKOTA CHILD

On the high oak wagon seat Hilda Mae
sat, small and erect beneath her
stubble colored straw hat, her bare
feet swinging above the golden wealth
in the wide Studebaker bed below.

"Unc" slapped the reins against the
horses' muscled rumps,"Giddap Coolie,
Bess, Wheat's two dollars a bushel."

Hilda Mae clung to the wooden bar
made to hold her in the seat.
Grandpa's warning rang a refrain
in her young minds ear,
"Never play in the wheat, it pulls
at you like quicksand."
She stretched her toes to barely
touch the soft kernels.

*Faded denims kept the burning sun
from Hilda Mae's short legs.
Americans had yet to learn the
German secret of blue dye.*

*Hilda Mae knew the flu had taken
mama, but her vocabulary was void
of those "half-world-away words",
adult words... Argonne, Chateau
Thierry and friendly sounding,
Big Bertha.*

*All she knew about the war was
holding grandma's hand beside a
flag draped casket, the sweet
scent of wild Dakota roses.*

*"We don't put sugar on our plums
so Belgian children can have food."*

*The four horse team, straining
under their sweat lathered
harness, urged the heavy wagon
forward.*

*Hilda Mae did not know Croesus
nor had she ever heard of Midas,
but hauling elevator wheat with
"Unc" this molten August day,
she was Queen of the Byzantine
on a twenty four karat bullion
throne and everything she touched
pure gold.*

KNUCKLE SHOTS

I hold my handful of hours
like worn glass marbles,
sorting. The polished taws
I lost in games of chance.

We played for 'keeps',
stakes ardent high
as our impassioned
hearts and willing lips.

I cherish now each
rough surviving 'dobie' and
fondle variegated 'aggies',
their deep veins faceted -
by calloused chips.

CUM GRANO SALUS

Why do the salt shakers at
the Hanford House
have larger holes than
those at Wendy's?

      The Romans paid their workmen
      with bags of salt.

Perhaps the nuclear engineers who
meet at the Hanford House
are worth more than the city employees
who grab a quick lunch at Wendy's.

      Our word salary comes from salt.

My grandmother let a guest
determine his or her own wealth
with the little glass dip at each plate.

At my aunt Vessie's table
my brother and I
were seated near the end
farthest from the host.

      Years later I learned we were
      "Below the salt".

When I eat at Wendy"s
I shake the cellar
    and shake
        and shake
           and shake.

RETIREMENT

*The lumps worn through by chafing time
have sifted into jeweled heap.*

*The sturdy reason, raucous rhyme,
have coalesced a shape to keep.*

*With dreams no longer clouds away
we stride the golden hours at hand*

*and gorge abbreviated days with
stuff to stay the slipping sand.*

PAPER BOY

*Up our ivy street
he rides as if he owns
the world,   this young
acne-ed entrepreneur who
whistles as he hurls the news.*

*By thirty feet he missed
the door yet adroitly executes
three 'wheelies' in our drive.*

*Unmindful of long paragraphs
that thrive on pestilence and
rumored war, he pedals by
each customer abode,
hails every barking dog
by name, but jauntily
ignores all residential
sidewalk code.*

STORM OVER THE UNION HALL

Dissent clashes between
flashes of lightning ire and
the rumbling, grumbling
opinions of thunder.

Raindrops hurled
from negotiations
bounce off streets and fields.

Demands, clouded
with hidden clauses,
bargain huff and bluff
over murky, inane causes.

Smoke-filled mediation yields
to evidence of sunlight,
melds all into a mutated
*   Logo of Rainbow.*

SPEECH IMPEDIMENT

When I was five, my stepmother told me,
"If you tell a lie, the Lord will split your tongue."
*   "Yes, mama."*

"The flowers? You picked the pansies?"
*   "Yes, mama."*

"The nuts? You ate the peanuts?"
*   "Yes, mama, every one."*

"Your swim suit -- it's dry?"
Tone clear and conscience clear,
*   "Yes, mama, I swam in the nude."*

Through time, she whacked my hands,
my mouth, my bottom, but the truth
kept my tongue intact.

"Last night? You spent it
with a girl friend?"
I kithed mama, yeth ith too hard to thay
with a thplit tongue.

BEING A DOG

I bay the moon
I yap after wheels
I growl at all things
unfamiliar.

Barking is my speech
My language is much more.

BLUE MOUNTAINS

Walk softly this Wallowa land!
Here spirit of Shoshone sleep.
The valiant Joseph and his band
of feathered warriors nightly keep
a phantom watch. The aspens speak
in whispers where the travois jolt
the dead - their medicine too weak
for white man's Winchester and Colt.

MEAL WITH ROBERT FROST

*It is a simple spread of fruit
from summer trees, brown bread
and cheese, with fish that only
hours ago had fought the line.
He draws his sustenance
for soul and mind and body
from these hard New England hills.
We talk and fill the afternoon
with silence in appropriate proportion.*

Before I go he reads.

*More than mere alchemy! I know
there is Power Divine
to make such miracle
of bread and wine.*

THE BIRTHDAY

*Today - he has not heard the musket shot
that split the April morning air.
He has not braved December night
to cross a freezing Delaware.
Today - his shoulders are not stooped beneath
responsibilities of a state,
nor does he dream that history
will someday honor him as great.
He has not heard the dying pray
for homes they will not see again
nor cries of "first in war, in peace, and
first in the hearts of countrymen."
He has not met young Lafayette
nor felt the cold of Valley Forge.
Today - a boy holds a new axe
beside a cherry tree.*

Happy birthday, George.

UPON BEING COMMITTED

Or maybe I was shoved.

I hear 'them' talking,
"Just another one who
fell through the cracks"
I feel no slivers, no barbs.

Could it have happened slowly
like sand flowing through the glass;
grain after grain, after final grain
before the hourly turning?

How could 'they' not know
the whole world has turned over and
I am the only one
      on top!

CLOCK RUN DOWN

*In senseless silence I awake
to unheard chimes.*

*The night is stopped where hands recount
across a dial - featured face
another time -
before the swinging motivation ceased.*

*Loose springs once coiled uptight, relax
in spiral ease.*

*The weights that regulate my day
rest in a deadlock and the balance stays
somewhere between the tick and tock.*

SNO-BOUND

*With the single-minded fervor
of a pioneer sod-buster
I will defend my urbanite
yard line.*

*No over-zealous broom or
snow-removal blade
shall invade this
polar privacy of mine.*

*Cross not that drifted barricade,
the silent white
that insulates my snug
cocoon of fire, book, and
steaming mug.*

*Nor trespass the deep winter night
to toss seed catalogues
across my gate
while January and I
hibernate.*

MAUDIE

At the frayed edge of fantasy
Maudie stroked the mange-infested cat.

> the social worker chided,
> "She never was a princess,
> in this life, or any other".

Worn-out Maudie pressed the purring
animal to her own fluttering heart.

> The daughter's words jack-hammered
> into Maudie's cluttered consciousness,
> "you don't remember things",
> "this is for your good",
> "face reality",
> "yes, put to sleep".

> Maudie's thin voice, "The money",
> trailed into a cough.
Social worker caught the magic phrase,

> "What money, you have money?"

> "Don't keep the driver waiting, mother."

"In the top bureau drawer, head of the stairs."
Princess licked at Maudie's withered hand.
"...a brown envelope; it's for the casket."

A TIME TO MOURN

Joe didn't cry
when his grandmother died,
nor did he shed a tear at her
funeral where distant relatives
wailed loud and long.
They called him a 'teenager
without feeling.'

Joe walked alone to the graying house
among the bark-shedding birches,
to the berry patch where Grandma
had worked a living before
her months of dieing.

*Joe was said to be
'not quite right in the head.'
His life had been sharing
and caring for the
aging woman.*

*He stopped to drink
at the rusty yard pump.
He lifted the familiar handle
slowly and quietly as he
had for weeks past so
there would be no grinding
screech to waken Grandma as she slept.
He had kept fresh water in her glass.*

No need for muted pumping now.

*Joe let the eager flood of clear,
cold water gush over his head,
his face, his hands in blend
with the torrent of tears too long
kept silent like the pump.*

SIX WHILE SNOWBOUND

Storm snow - breaks limbs,
downs wires, and gives a facelift
to my Chevrolet.

Flakes - like swan feathers
flutter from white sky to earth
equalizing lawns.

Feigning innocence,
snowdrift's proffer promises,
caress bent fenders.

Sunshine and ice drape
rhinestone spangles and lame'
around our garbage.

January snow
covers the orchard with love
for next year's apples.

Beneath soft blankets
of snow, wheat seeds germinate
await birth in spring.

HOUSE FIRE

The warped and blackened beams,
 tortured by last night's flame and water,
list precariously on unstable studs.

Iron casters mark old territorial rights
 of bed and chiffonnier.

A twisted wire holds shards
 of broken glass and memories.

Cold, fickle ashes shift above a latent ember,
 awaiting only one deriding gust
  to burst again into remembered conflagration.

WHITE SWAN SCHOOL

*This is his season -
a sometime summer
shaped for him
by the Great God-Spirit,
not for straight sitting
with a cipher slate
shut in a place
with this pale chatterer,
but cosmic still to wait
the whir of feathers
flushed from thick
sumac and salal.*

*Beyond the hazy alphabet he knows
the huckleberries hang
pulp purple in the last
September sun.
How could she tell him of the wars,
who won, who fell?
Her great-grandfather
wasn't chief and
Isaac Stevens is a name
that he will never
need to spell.*

P.O.W. WIFE

She pursues sleep through
a maze of dreams,
wakens to a birdsong reveille
and the gnawing of
not knowing.

As black coffee steams
she musters thoughts that feed
themselves like vermin in Bastille
When, mad from hunger,
chewed upon their own tails.

She has no crusading shield
against such unseen foe,
her dreams worn thin as pre-war
tires and a marriage in limbo
she races with the rat routine
counterplot of patriotism.

TRADING POST

Behind a garish front
he hucks his sundry wares.
A dusty bulb illumines
twisting lanes between
the pyramids of chairs,
beds, bottles and old magazines -
residual from years of bartering.

The brazen clang of cowbell
on the door rings in
each customer with
caste-less cold indifference
and bargaining begins -
price-sparring,
"special", "deal", "friend".
Each seeker feels he
bested in the end.

Antiquers come to probe
among the piles of pots,
(iron is so collectible).
To the girl who brought
her gold to trade; spectacles,
some wedding bands,
he answers, "pound for pound",
and scans her offering.

The clapper sounds again
its unmelodious strain.
She pushes, closes, staggers,
beneath her weight of gain.

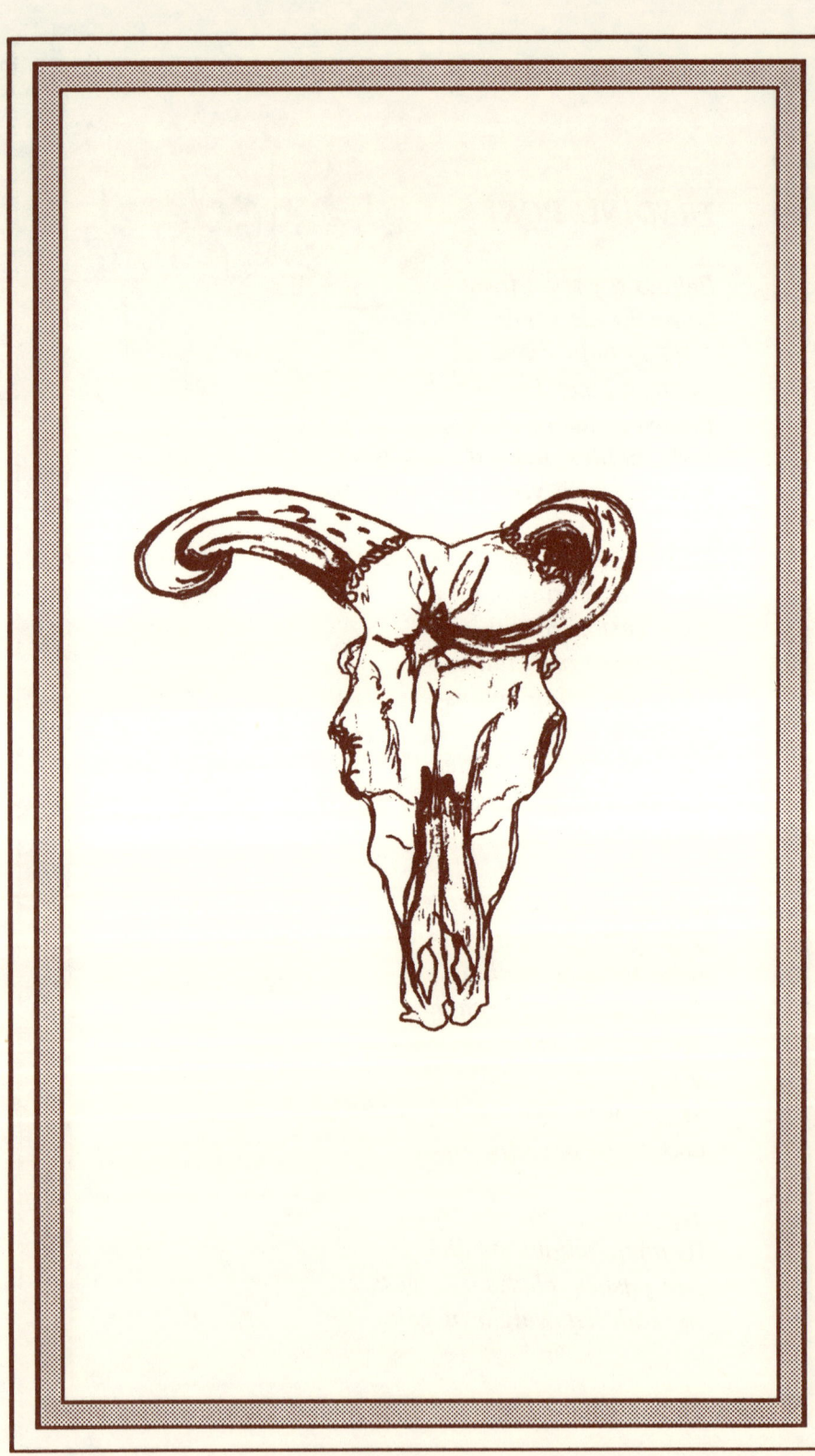

CAUTERIZATION

*When I was twelve, I was gored in the leg
by a bull. A generation of fear followed.*

*My son of twelve took a calf to raise.
I resolved to remove the pliable buttons
which would harden and shape into horns.
Through the growing time
I sawed, I burned, I medicated.*

*One day the steer attacked the boy.
A horn not allowed to grow outward
had penetrated the animal brain and
madness surely followed.*

WHEAT LAND

*When undulating fields of golden grain
fuse to a raw sienna sky,
horizons press with firmament. Where Heaven
begins is indiscernible to the eye.*

*In years of summer drought,
and mark this well,
the same can easily
be said of Hell!*

SONG OF THE COLUMBIA

I am Shining Water -

There was no time in my beginning,
        Only sunrise and sunset.
Years and centuries were as sands
        Rolling from a hillside
Continuous, beginning as one
        Until so many came
The whole of pre-historic
        Faded into oblivion.
There was no eye to marvel
        At the sunrise splendor
In ethereal sky and clear water:
        No ear to catch the sound
Of rushing, splashing, pushing
        Into an ever widening river
Wearing it way to the sea.

I am Shining Water -

The salmon came: The Red man fished
        And built a boat, a bow
And arrow to bring down game
        For food and dress. Great tribes
Would gather for the hunt and though
        Indian traveled far to Eastern Plain
For buffalo and deer, he always
        Found the pathway led
Back to my shore.

I am Shining Water -

Great mountains rumbled to themselves
    Then threw their fiery bowels
Into the sky. The atmosphere
    Was black with smoke and ashes.
Tall trees tumbled. Earth and rock gave 'way.
    When all was quiet some of
The Mountain Gods were gone. Others
    Were smaller than before.
The river flowed on.

I am Shining Water -

White man came from the sea
    And over the mountains.
There were guns, - and Bibles,
    Covered wagons, and women,
Children, homes, and gardens.
    Civilization crowed the shores,
Conquered the wildness of the mountain,
    The loneliness of the desert.

I am Shining Water -

Villages grew into towns
    And towns into cities.
A few stores in a farming community
    became a project for world peace.
Thousands came, a trailer city came,
    a trailer city settled on my shores,
Still through desert, age-old basalt
    And mountain, I flow, flow, flow,
From eternity into eternity.

I am Shining Water

UPON FINDING AN AIRPLANE PROPELLER

IN A

JAPANESE ANTIQUE SHOP

I was prepared to pay her more,
but five was all she asked.
    "It isn't old, you know -
    from World War 2".
Not old to her. She had her years
of laughter before 'Pearl'.
To me, who never knew my father,
it was life.

We pulled to wrench it from the clutter.
She feared I might break something
if I tugged at it alone.
Break what,
the cracked showcase
of a mid-Victorian age, the Georgian silver
that somehow survived the tarnish
and the dust?

*Since Empire furniture is
difficult to move and patterned glass calls to
a more discerning eye,
the graciousness of the shop had years ago
descended to debris.
A curtain partially concealed the ante-room
that held her meal and cot.*

> *The laminated wood yielded to her
> yellow parchment hands.
> We pulled it free.
> My flesh crawled with cold of an
> infamous December day.
> A numbness precessed into flight.
> Corregidor
> and perspiration of a jungle night.*

*I clutched the wooden form that once
had drawn me from the street and
wrestled it as Jacob did his dream
until control was mine.*

*I held it at arm's length and from
the shape of sinewed softness to
the disciplined brass edge,*

> *I brushed accumulation
> of the years.*

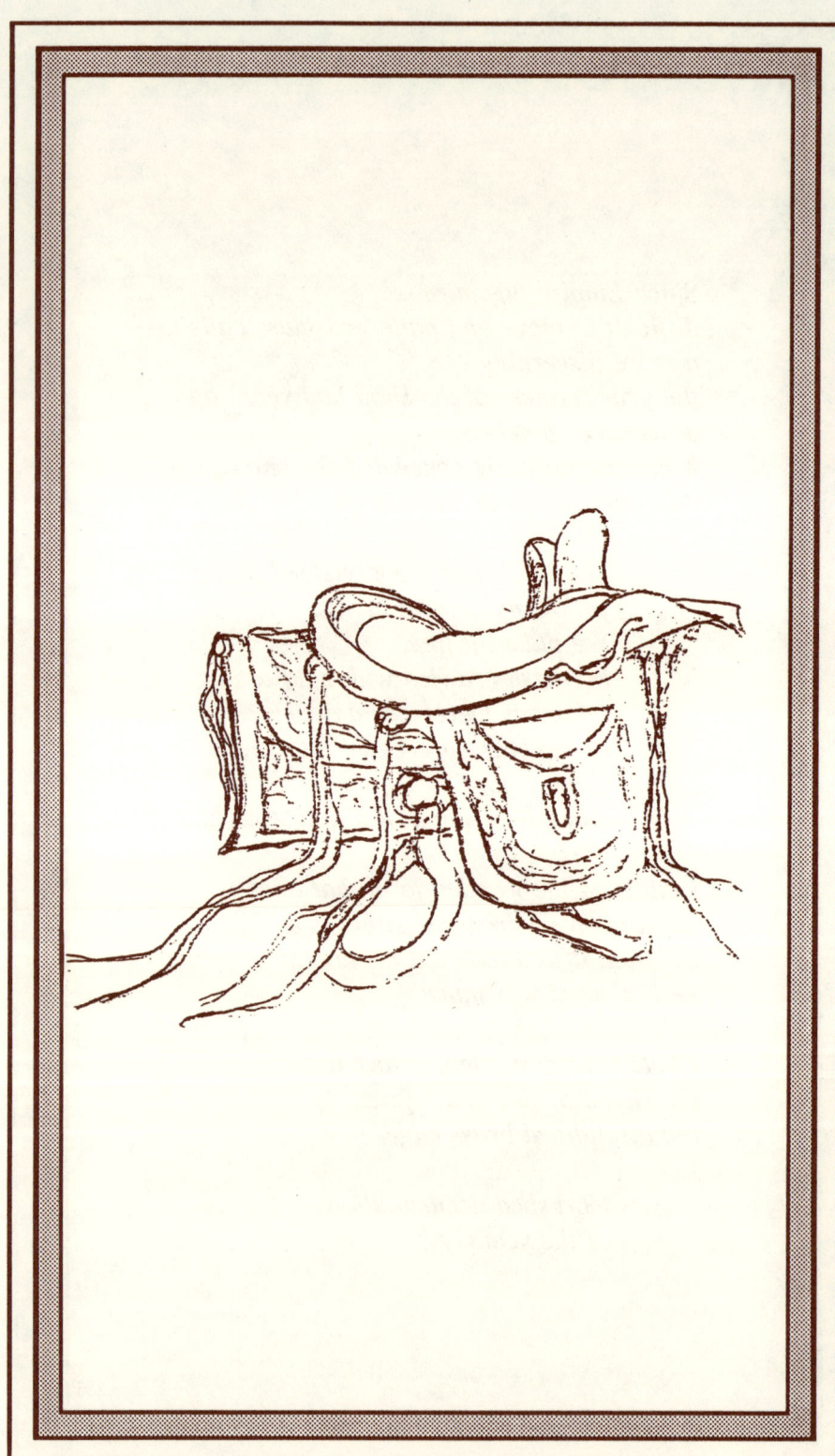

GREAT AUNT HARRIET

She rode life
sidesaddle

as on a gaited horse,
ramrod straight
with matching virtue.

We watched in awe
her art of equitation,
straps held by so small a hand.

Aunt Harriet knew;
one slack rein,
the animal could jump
from her control.

SOJOURNERS

Sunday morning snow had glazed our street
with a sparkling sugar icing.

The elderly Shaws
were first to venture out,
releasing their Mercedes
across the glittering unlined lanes.
He carefully slid a right curve
toward their uptown cathedral.

Then came Mr. and Mrs. Wilson
in a brown station wagon
alive with assorted five
young Wilsons.
The vehicle eased straight
forward to the corner stop,
urged ahead by the winter
tone of a ringing bell.

The Moto neighbors
weren't far behind.
She, holding close
the blanket bundle,
not trusting her baby
to a belted seat.

*Young, proud husband
guided the holiday-red Toyota
into a left turn that led
the way to the shrine
of their choice.*

*Our street, now compromised
by contours of patterned tracks,
looked safe. I manipulated
my own four wheels
toward our brick church,
with its lighted cross
on the steeple.*

*So many diverse ways,
paths, trails, courses; yet
each traveler hoping to
eventually arrive at
the same destination.*

THE WYE MARKET

Where highways 85 and 60 meet
the asphalts weld huge waves of heat
that buckle into one.
The line of lanes is inundated as the
melting colors run.
The tangled cables swing their load
of systematic lights to timely
blink decisions to the road,
a stop, a left, a right or go-ahead
its shimmering mirage
of green and red.

    Here the Wye Market stands
    or sprawls in a disheveled scar
    like wounded fungus
    on the land triangular.
    The washed fruit, vegetables, cold pop
    and souvenirs vie in their disarray
    to catch the tourist eye.

At the lean-to's rear, discarded
truck tarpaulins weave
a partial shade along the make-shift wall.
Fluorescent messages, risque and
plagiarized from everywhere,
fade in the fly-specked day.

*The plastic lugs of corpulent tomatoes shrink
from morning-full to
mere two-thirds by afternoon.
A fan disturbs the stagnant air
in oscillating monotone.
The summer wasp and honey-bee contrive
to aggravate skin punctures and explore
a cache of sugar in an over-ripened pear.*

Ammonia steams from dampened sawdust on the floor
where a French Poodle reprobate has
smelled the squash in tour.
Long stalks of aromatic dill and fiery red
hot peppers hang suspended overhead.

    Out front,
mutated tapestries
    with strident scarlet flowers bloom
    velvet over sagging clothesline wire.

Acrylic elk and deer together
in a chartreuse forest run and
bound by a tangled fringe

    *A lone discounted Christ
hangs bleeding in the sun.*

ADDICT

I ran until all breath was gone.
Always beyond my reach the bird flew on.
He swooped, he veered, he rose
before my uncoordinated hands
could close around him.
An old man called,
"Put salt upon his tail."
one final fall along the shifting shale,
the bird was mine - a morbid thing,
talons tearing flesh,
black wings absorbing every light,
his evil vulture eye disgracing night
to keep my soul embalmed.
I gestured love -
He spit his putrid carrion upon my arm.

LANCASTER COUNTY

Between them in a small pine box,
plain and hand-hewn, their firstborn lay.

She longed to touch John's strengthening hand.
She hoped that he would sense her need.
Her John, his bearded face too stern for
twenty years, stared half-seeing down the road;
nor slackened his firm grip upon the reins.

Her fingers traced the promises within the Book.
Comfort seemed to flow from these worn words.

The Book had been her mother's
and her mother's mother's.

She sat stiff in the wooden seat, the boards
unyielding as the faith.
It was His will; She could not question this.

Yet one so small should not be called
before he'd known the warmth
of summer mud between his toes;
before she'd had a chance to fill a pail
for him of sugar-cakes and liverwurst
to swing to school,
or head cheese from the weighted crock.

She smoothed again the starched black
bonnet on her head.
Less with her lips than with her heart
she formed the words,

"A mighty fortress is our God."

INTERVAL

Those "V" shaped lines
of soaring wings that cry
the straggler on
or haggle over flight plans
in a steel November sky
can surely feel
this fall is not the same
as other autumns
when a boy, a gun, and
flying geese were all a game
to play like hide and seek
in decoyed blinds.

You've taught him well
those lessons he so needs
to know, of changing course
and spiraling through clouds
to dodge the death
from swamps below.

Today is yours.

Skim low and barely clear
the cliff. Throw caution
to the winds

For sure as seasons come
and go he will be back
to call you in through fog.
He'll tramp free his
beloved shores and hills
when geese and boy and gun
again will be a game.

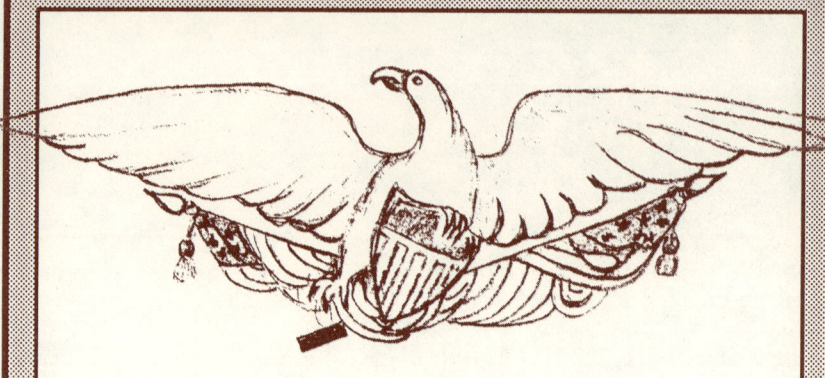

CLE ELUM - NOVEMBER 11, 1918

*At eleven o'clock
we tied the mine whistle down.
for one hour the blast blew;
the mill alarm, church bells,
fire sirens, and horns.
Pandemonium crowded the street,
shouts in Italian, Hungarian,
Polish, Slavic, but all
American.*

*New stars and stripes waved
from second story windows.
First generation patriots
proudly part of an
Armistice, a war
to end all wars.
My father's thick voice
broken by tears,
"This is our land."*

*Above the family Bible
in the parlor we
hung my brother's helmet.*

IMAGES

Summer's on the block
    "Going, going,
The raspberry bush flaunts
its final rust sweet fruit
A touch and it falls
into my cupped hand.
Mother Nature drops the gavel
    "Gone."

A sharp cut of breeze
jumps on the bandwagon,
urging forward the last
sporadic spell of warmth
as summer halts and falters
the parade.
    "Move on, or in a shout
    of mocking cheers, bow out."

The season barters
    "One more lazy day"
like a truant youngster
lingering on the schoolhouse step,
procrastinating
his unknown answers
to a baffling cipher sum.

Summer is a favored poem
I"ve read it many times -
three score, more,
from its blustery beginning,
knowing as my senses squander
those trite, cherished rhymes,
to the last dim, tear-eroded line.

To a Lecture

I came with a friend,
Subject: Carassius Auratus
My friend has an aquarium.

I do not have an aquarium,
       I do not want an aquarium
nor do I wish to know about pet fish.

People were arriving
chattering in unmetered monotone.

Introductions
with sugared accolades.

Colored slides.

The speaker droned,
       "Japanese domesticated the carp
       in the sixteenth century.
       They bred them down to
       the small yellow fish of today."

I dozed.

       "A goldfish adapts its size to
       the size of its container."

I opened one eye.
       "A two inch fish will never
       outgrow a four inch bowl."

I opened both eyes.
       "Whereas a goldfish
       dropped into a river
       will increase to many times
       its original size."

I listened.

Listening lets me swim
in a wider stream.

AFTER A VISIT FROM A GRANDAUGHTER

*Suspicious of the quietness,
the cat creeps out
from underneath a chair.
He arches past the rumpled dolls
and stretches on the baby bonnet
he was forced to wear.*

*I settle back to sterile calm
with kettle, tea
and loneliness that shows
through all my ordered discipline.
The cat just purrs and licks
at bubblegum between his toes.*

ACCOUNTING BEFORE BREAKFAST

*I add, subtract, and
search for assets hidden
in the flexibility of ink.
Joggers pass my window, east,
their shadows shuttering
the sunrise with closely
calculated dashes on
my debit sheet.*

*The silver gulls flash
escalating flight forms
to my ledger as
they zero in on
overly extended worms.*

*Black coffee breaks
monotony of minuses, and
golden upper brackets
of the sky secure a
solvent day ahead.*

*Still, the balance of the night
is streaked with red.*

TO THE KIDNEY BANK

Moved by your plea
In tonight's news and
Being of sound mind
And body, I choose
To will to you my kidneys.
Then
Snug in my last sleep
Somewhere between
this mirth of earth
And the Beyond
I shall rest each 6 a.m.
Serene
Knowing that another
In his saturated waking
Hurries down a hall
To the latrine.

HOAR FROST

*With silver ribbon
and with tinsel
you have tied
the stream where summer
fishes swim and shiver
deep inside.*

*How clever is your
glittered lettering
that ices ivy and
the once-green everything
with, "Please, do not open until spring."*

TO JIM

*In some clandestine dark
upon a borrowed bed
tell her how misunderstood
you are, how beautiful
your need -
Promise her a ring and
after our divorce
the bells and rice -
in this unholy hour, before
the cock crows
twice.*

*If your highway spreads
a disappointing mirage ahead,*

Stop! and swim in it.

ROAD FROM RENO

*Into the shimmering
unshape of mirage,
I move,
as one detached,
not part of the
uncertainty ahead;
yet alien also
to the rear view
mirrored lanes.
For love
and yesterday
no eulogy is said -
no stone.
The desert of
dissolved togetherness
so soon
reclaims its own.*

THE OLD ROAD MOTEL

*The 'come-on' is a lack
of flashing neon light;
"Off-highway beds", seclusion
for rest of night.*

*Vine maples grow undisciplined.
The false facade
is stripped, exposing cheap
undress beyond the shade.*

*The Cabots and the Lowells
seldom intrude,
but here for years, sequestered
Smiths have rendezvoused.*

THE BALLAD OF WILLIE KEIL

November covered a coffin gray,
against the jack pines on the hill,
as shovels split primeval clay
to shape a grave for Willie Keil.

No lumbering wheels intrude upon
the silence of his sacred rest.
Three thousand miles dead Willie rode
a Conestoga rolling west.

His father, Dr. William Keil,
was leader of the Bethel band,
whose pious pilgrims pushed their faith
across an unconverted land.

Missouri winter tempered plans
and disciplined departure date.
For Willie, just nineteen, it was
a harsh, uncompromising wait.

Supplies were ready for the trek,
the animals, the food, the grain.
Stern elders promised Will that he
could drive the first team of the train.

When April melted into May,
the sad 'goodbyes' were fondly said,
but just four days before they left,
a fever struck poor Willie dead.
The conscience of the colony;
the men were grave, the women wept,
decided to take Will along,
a promise made was a promise kept.

Late into night the hammers rang.
A box was fashioned, lined with lead,

filled with corn whiskey, and in this
they placed the body of their dead.

A seal of beeswax set the lid.
New rawhide tied it to the seat.
The wagons rolled, the members sang
a lament dirge of no retreat.

As westward the procession moved,
fierce Indian wars raged through the land,
though other trains were massacred,
no ill befell this holy band.

Smoke signals spiraled to the sky,
warned Sioux, Shoshone and Cayuse.
From tribe to tribe the message told
of a ghost driver; memaloos.

As summer months dragged into fall,
through dust and flood they pressed their way
'til prairies passed and mountains scaled,
they found the place where they would stay.

In Washington, near Auburn town,
so you may find this story real,
a marker stands to point the grave
of our beloved Willie Keil.

BREAK-UP

*Possessed by ice
the river throbs and moves
within its sphere
to a more compromising season.
Floes of fractured
whiteness split the air
and frenzied current
spreads undisciplined
to beds
of least resistance.*

HEIRLOOMS

*Grandmother Wright
has three glass compotes,
beautiful,
blown into molds and
pressed with design
while the glass was pliable.*

*We use them with every
Sunday dinner, where
after church,
the sermon is discussed.
Grandfather carves:
"Serve from the left,
take up from the right."*

*I ask Grandmother,
"why are these compotes
special?"
"Because, although the molds
that shaped them are gone,
the intricate patterns
endure."*

AFTER ELECTION

Invigorating is to hear,
"Good Morning," without
the tilted tongue of party politics,
a sincere, "How are you?"
with smiles not twisted into,
"Yea" or "Nay"

I am for sunshine, yet
I will not picket rain.

Today I'll sip hot tea
with, sugar, lemon, and
the cream of cordiality,
warm company of a friend,

Enjoying, knowing that
four years from now
we will be on
"Non speaking"
terms again.

SERENITY IN SEPTEMBER

*In a lazy hammock
under a drowsy willow tree
I watch an undecided leaf
flirt coyly with a breeze.*

*Through my fantasizing ear
I hear,
"Shall I fall for this young zephyr blade
or cling to the host twig until a more
experienced gigolo comes gusting
in a whirlwind escapade to throw me
        spinning,
                reeling,
                       falling
giddy to earth's unfeeling floor?"*

*An opportunist sparrow
searching for a tasty treat
pecked at a juicy slug on the stem,
just right for him to eat.*

*With spiral ease the leaf descended,
landed, resting on my page of poetry.*

I closed the book.

*Some future lyric dreamer
lounging out an autumn afternoon
with Keats and Shelley while
letting time erode
will wonder at a broken leaf
long pressed between a skylark sonnet
and a Grecian ode.*

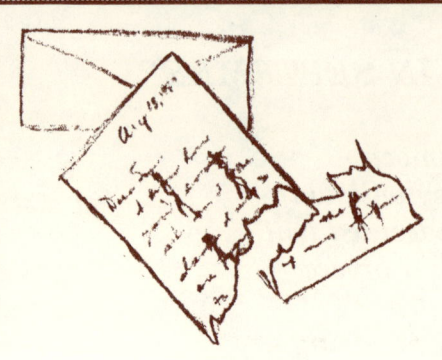

PERPETUITY

To my heirs:

*I can't take them with me,
my verses and quips
so after my leaving
don't
waste your time grieving
you'll still be receiving
rejection slips.*

NOTES

NOTES